Published by

Balaji

Title: Samosa

Purchase my books online from:

Amazon

THE AUTHOR

Ji saays

CONTENT

Sweet Potato Samosa

Peas Samosa

Vegetable Samosa

Punjabi Samosa

Cashew Samosa

Fruit Samosa

Moong Dal Samosa

Chickpeas Samosa

Cabbage Samosa

Mini Samosa

Paneer Samosa

Samosa Chaat

Peas and Paneer Samosa

Broccoli Samosa

Methi Samosa

Wheat Samosa

Spinach Vegetable

Moong Sprouts Samosa

Crispy Paneer Samosa

Cauliflower Samosa

Sweet Samosa

Mushroom Samosa

Cocktail Samosas

Samosa

Sweet Potato Samosa

Ingredients:

Maida (Plain Flour) – 400 Gms

Warm Water – 200ml

Oil – 1/4 cup + some more for frying

Salt – 2 tsp

For the Filling:

Green Peas – 200 Gms

Sweet Potatoes – 2 big or 4 medium, peeled, chopped

Onions – 2, big, chopped

Garlic – 3 cloves, crushed

Oil – 1/2 cup

Ginger – 2 inch piece, grated

Red Chilli Powder – 4 tsp (adjust as per taste)

Green Chillies – 4, chopped, seeds removed

Coriander Leaves – few, chopped

Salt as per taste

Method:

1. Mix the flour, 1/4 cup of oil, water and salt in a bowl.

2. Knead well and cover the bowl.

3. Keep aside for 30 to 45 minutes.

4. Heat 1/4 cup of oil in a pan.

5. Add the onions, ginger, garlic and green chillies.

6. Saute well for a minute.

7. Add the sweet potatoes and reduce flame to low.

8. Cook until the potatoes are cooked, stirring often.

9. If needed add a little water to prevent the potatoes from sticking to the bottom of the pan.

10. Add the green peas and cook for 3 to 5 minutes.

11. Add the coriander leaves, salt, red chilli powder and stir well.

12. Remove from flame and allow it to cool slightly.

13. Make medium balls of the dough and roll them into a thin circle.

14. Add some of the filling and fold into a triangle. Cut the excess dough and use them again.

15. Brush the edges with a little water and seal the samosas.

16. Heat oil in a deep frying pan over medium flame.

17. Gently add the samosas and cook for 10 to 15 minutes or until light golden brown.

18. Remove and drain excess oil.

19. Serve hot with chutney or sauce.

Peas Samosa

Ingredients:

Maida – 1 cup

Oil – 2 tblsp

Salt as per taste

Oil for frying

For the filling:

Onions – 1 cup, chopped

Peas – 1/4 cup

Salt as per taste

Chaat Masala Powder – 1/4 tsp

Ginger Garlic Paste – 1/4 tsp

Green Chilli Paste – 1/4 tsp

Saunf – 1/4 tsp

Oil – 3 tsp

Coriander Leaves – few, chopped

Mint Leaves – few, chopped

Method:

1. Mix the maida, 2 tblsp oil and salt in a bowl to a thick, pliable dough.

2. Heat 3 tsp oil in a pan over medium flame.

3. Add the saunf and fry for 20 seconds.

4. Add the onions and saute until golden.

5. Add the remaining filling ingredients and mix well.

6. Cook for a minute and remove from flame.

7. Make small balls of the dough and roll them into small/medium puris.

8. Add 1 or 2 tblsp of the filling and fold into a triangle.

9. Seal the edges using little water.

10. Heat oil in a deep frying pan over medium flame.

11. Fry the prepared samosas until light golden brown.

12. Remove and drain excess oil.

13. Serve hot with chutney or sauce.

Vegetable Samosa

Ingredients:

Maida – 500 Gms

Potatoes – 500 Gms, quartered

Green Peas – 100 Gms, shelled

Onions – 100 Gms, finely chopped

Ginger Paste – 1 tblsp

Green Chilli Paste – 1 tblsp

Turmeric Powder – 1 tsp

Cashew Nuts – 15 to 20, broken (optional)

Cumin Seeds – 1 to 2 tsp

Saunf – 1 to 2 tsp

Coriander Leaves – handful, chopped

Garam Masala Powder – 2 tsp

Butter – 50 Gms

Salt as per taste

Oil as required

Method:

1. Add a little salt to peas and potatoes.

2. Add enough water and pressure cook until 1 whistle.

3. Remove and drain well. Reserve the water.

4. Melt butter and add to a large bowl.

5. Add maida, salt, cumin powder and enough water.

6. Knead well to a Poori dough consistency.

7. Make small balls and roll them out.

8. Heat little oil in a pan.

9. Fry the saunf for 20 seconds.

10. Add onions, cashew nuts, green chilli paste, ginger paste, turmeric powder, garam masala powder and stir well.

11. Add the potatoes (peel before adding) and green peas.

12. Cook for 2 to 3 minutes and mash lightly.

13. Add coriander leaves and mix again.

14. Remove from flame and allow it to cool slightly.

15. Add 1 or 2 tblsp of the potato mixture to the rolled out puris.

16. Fold them into a triangle and shape into a samosa.

17. Heat oil in a deep frying pan over medium flame.

18. Fry the prepared samosas until light golden brown.

19. Remove and drain excess oil.

20. Serve with mint chutney or sauce.

Punjabi Samosa

Ingredients:

Maida – 2 cups

Ghee – 3 tblsp

Salt – 2 tsp or as per taste

Oil for frying

For the Filling:

Green peas – 1 cup, boiled, lightly mashed

Potatoes – 3 to 4, big, boiled, peeled, mashed

Pomegranate Seeds – 2 tsp, dried (optional)

Coriander Seeds – 2 tblsp

Cumin Seeds – 2 tsp

Oil – 3 to 4 tblsp

Ginger – 2 inch piece, peeled, chopped

Green Chillies – 5 to 6, chopped

Red Chilli Powder – 2 tsp

Dried Mango Powder (Amchoor) – 2 tsp

Garam Masala Powder – 2 tsp

Salt as per taste

Coriander Leaves – handful, chopped

Method:

1. Combine the ghee, salt and maida in a large bowl.

2. Add 1/2 cup of warm water and knead well to stiff dough.

3. Cover with a damp cloth and keep aside for 20 to 30 minutes.

4. Heat a pan over medium flame.

5. Dry roast the coriander seeds and dried pomegranate seeds for 45 to 90 seconds.

6. Remove, cool and grind to a coarse powder.

7. Add oil to the pan.

8. Fry the cumin seeds until lightly browned.

9. Add the ginger and green chillies.

10. Fry for 45 to 60 seconds.

11. Add the coriander-pomegranate powder, red chilli powder, dried mango powder, garam masala powder and salt.

12. Mix well.

13. Add the peas and potatoes.

14. Mix again and cook for 5 to 10 minutes.

15. Add coriander leaves and stir again.

16. Remove from flame.

17. Make small balls of the dough and roll them into a small puri.

18. Add 1 or 2 tblsp of the filling and fold into samosa.

19. Seal the edges with a little water.

20. Heat oil for deep frying over medium flame.

21. Fry the prepared samosa for 5 to 8 minutes or until golden brown and crisp.

22. Remove and drain excess oil.

23. Serve hot as a snack with chutney or sauce.

Cashew Samosa

Ingredients:

Maida – 2 cups

Sugar – 1 cup

Cashews – 1 cup

Coconut – 1 cup, grated

Cardamom Powder – 2 tsp

Oil as required

Method:

1. Combine maida, salt and enough water.

2. Knead well to a pliable dough.

3. Combine the cashews, coconut, cardamom powder, sugar and grind together in a mixie.

4. Make small puris of the dough and add 2 to 3 tblsp of the cashew mixture.

5. Fold well and shape into a samosa.

6. Heat oil for frying and fry the prepared samosas.

7. Remove and drain excess oil.

8. Sprinkle some sugar on top and serve at once.

Fruit Samosa

Ingredients:

Maida – 2 cups

Ghee – 2 tblsp

Bananas – 2 cups, chopped

Dates – 2 cups, finely chopped

Mace Powder – 1/2 tsp

Orange Juice – 2 tblsp

Method:

1. Combine the fruits, mace powder and orange juice in a bowl.

2. Mix ghee, maida and enough water in another bowl and knead well to a pliable dough.

3. Make small puris and add 2 tblsp of the fruit mixture.

4. Fold into a triangle and seal the edges with little water.

5. Heat a flat tawa over medium flame.

6. Place the prepared samosas and apply ghee around the edges.

7. Cook on both sides until golden.

8. Remove and serve at once.

Moong Dal Samosa

Ingredients:

Wheat Flour – 2 cups

Moong Dal – 2 cups, boiled, lightly mashed

Pepper Powder – 2 tsp

Salt as per taste

Oil as required

Method:

1. Combine the dal, pepper powder and little salt in a bowl.

2. Mix well.

3. Add salt and enough water to wheat flour.

4. Knead well to a chapati dough consistency.

5. Make small puris and add 1 or 2 tblsp of the dal mixture.

6. Fold well into a triangle.

7. Heat oil for deep frying.

8. Fry the prepared samosas until golden brown.

9. Remove and drain excess oil.

10. Serve with sauce or chutney.

Chickpeas Samosa

Ingredients:

Maida – 2 cups

Ghee – 2 tblsp

White Chickpeas – 1 to 2 cups, boiled, lightly mashed

Coconut – 2 tblsp

Green Chilli Paste – 2 to 3 tsp

Salt as per taste

Oil as required

Method:

1. Mix the chickpeas, coconut and green chilli paste in a bowl.

2. Combine maida, ghee, salt and little water in a bowl.

3. Knead well to a puri dough consistency.

4. Make small puris and add 1 to 2 tblsp of the chickpeas mixture.

5. Fold and shape into a triangle.

6. Heat oil in a deep frying pan.

7. Fry the prepared samosa until golden brown.

8. Remove and serve hot with chutney or sauce.

Cabbage Samosa

Ingredients:

Maida – 1 cup

Cabbage – 1/2 cup, finely chopped

Green Peas – 1 tblsp, shelled

Ginger – 1 tblsp, finely grated

Spring Onions – 1 tblsp

Soy Sauce – 1 tblsp

Pepper Powder – 1 tsp

Salt as per Tate

Oil as required

Method:

1. Add salt and little water to maida.

2. Knead well.

3. Mix the cabbage, peas, spring onions, soy sauce and pepper powder in a bowl.

4. Make small balls of the dough and roll them into small puris.

5. Add 1 or 2 tblsp of the cabbage filling and fold into a triangle.

6. Heat oil in a deep frying pan.

7. Gently slide the prepared samosas and fry until golden brown.

8. Remove and drain excess oil.

9. Serve hot with chutney or sauce.

Mini Samosa

Ingredients:

Maida – 250 Gms

Ghee – 150 Gms

Oil

Salt as per taste

For the Filling:

Potatoes – 4, boiled and mashed

Onion – 1, finely chopped (optional)

Cinnamon – 1/2 tsp

Oil – 4 tsp

Ajwain (Carom Seeds) – 1/4 tsp

Salt as per taste

Method:

1. Heat oil in a pan.

2. Add the mashed potatoes, onions, cinnamon, carom seeds and salt.

3. Stir-fry for 2 to 3 minutes.

4. Keep aside.

5. Sift together the maida, salt and ghee

6. Mix well till it resembles breadcrumbs.

7. Add just enough water to knead into a dough.

8. Divide the dough into 12 to 14 portions.

9. Roll out each portion into a very thin chapatti.

10. Cut 3 inches broad strips from each chapatti so as to get 2 to 3 such strips.

11. Pick up one strip at a time.

12. Place a portion of the filling in the centre of the strip and roll over the filling 3 to 4 times so that the final product is a triangular shaped samosa with various layers.

13. Prepare samosa from the different strips.

14. Roll out another portion and again cut into strips and prepare the layered samosas in this way.

15. Heat oil in a pan on medium heat.

16. Fry the samosas a few at a time so that these are crispy and golden brown.

17. Serve hot with chutney or sauce

Paneer Samosa

Ingredients:

Paneer – 250 Gms, finely chopped

Maida – 2 cups

Onion – 1, finely chopped

Green Chillies – 2, finely chopped

Red Chilli Powder – 1 tsp

Cumin Seeds – 1/2 tsp

Lemon Juice – 1 tsp

Butter – 50 Gms, melted

Salt as per taste

Oil as required

Method:

1. Combine the maida, butter and salt in a bowl.

2. Mix well to a puri dough consistency.

3. Heat a little oil in a pan.

4. Fry the cumin seeds for 30 seconds.

5. Add the onions, green chillies and saute for a minute or two.

6. Add red chilli powder, lemon juice, salt and paneer.

7. Mix well and stir-fry for a minute.

8. Remove from flame.

9. Make small balls of the dough and roll them in small/medium puris.

10. Shape the prepared puris into cones and add 1 or 2 tblsp of the paneer mixture.

11. Fold and seal the edges with little water.

12. Heat oil in a deep frying pan.

13. Fry the prepared samosas until golden.

14. Remove and drain excess oil.

15. Serve hot with chutney or ketchup.

Samosa Chaat

Ingredients:

Maida – 1 cup

Oil – 2 tblsp

Salt – a pinch

Baking Powder – a pinch

Cold Water as required

Oil as required for frying

For the filling:

Onions – 2, finely chopped

Potatoes – 2, boiled, mashed

Carrot – 2 tblsp, finely chopped

Green Peas – 100 Gms

Beans – 10, finely chopped, boiled

Salt as per taste

Garam Masala Powder as per taste

Green Chillies – 1, chopped

Cumin Powder – 1/2 tsp

Oil as required

To garnish:

Thick Curd – 1 cup

Chaat Masala Powder – as required

Sev as required

Sweet Tamarind Chutney as required

Green Chutney as required

Coriander Leaves – few, chopped

Onion – 1/4 cup, finely chopped (or as required)

Cucumber – 1/4 cup, finely chopped

Green Chillies – 2 to 3, finely chopped

Method:

1. To make the samosas, mix the maida, 2 tblsp oil, salt, baking powder in a bowl.

2. Add enough cold water and mix well.

3. Cover with a damp cloth for 30 minutes.

4. Meanwhile heat little oil in a pan.

5. Saute the onions and green chillies for a minute.

6. Add the potatoes, carrots, green peas, beans, garam masala powder and cumin powder.

7. Mix well and add salt.

8. Keep aside in a bowl.

9. Make small balls of the dough and roll them into small puris.

10. Add 1 or 2 tblsp of the filling and fold well into a samosa.

11. Heat oil in a deep frying pan over medium flame.

12. Cook the prepared samosas until cooked and golden.

13. Remove and drain excess oil.

14. Transfer to a serving plate and crush them lightly.

15. Garnish with curd, sweet tamarind chutney, green chutney, chaat masala powder, onions, green chillies, cucumber, sev and coriander leaves on top.

16. Serve at once.

Peas and Paneer Samosa

Ingredients:

Paneer – 100 Gms, cubed

Potatoes – 100 Gms, boiled, peeled, mashed

Onion – 1, chopped

Mint Leaves – 1 tblsp, chopped

Green Peas – 1/4 cup, thawed if frozen

Garam Masala Powder – 1 tblsp

Mango Chutney – 1 to 2 tblsp, available in most major stores (optional)

Red Chilli Powder – 1/4 tsp

Pastry Sheets – 1 pack

Butter – 1/2 to 3/4 cup, melted

Juice and Zest of 1 small Lemon

Oil – as required

Salt as per taste

Method:

1. Heat little oil in a pan over medium flame.

2. Fry the paneer cubes until golden.

3. Add the chopped onions, mint leaves, chilli powder and garam masala powder.

4. Saute for a minute or two.

5. Remove and transfer to a bowl.

6. Add the mashed potatoes, green peas, juice and zest of lemon and mango chutney.

7. Add a little salt (if desired) and mix well.

8. Keep aside.

9. Separate the pastry sheets and brush them lightly with the melted butter. Cut them in half if required.

10. Add 1 tblsp of the potato-paneer mixture to one end of the sheet.

11. Fold over, covering the mixture, to make a triangle.

12. Keep folding until you reach the end of the sheet.

13. Brush the edges with some more butter and seal tightly.

14. Heat oil in a deep frying pan over medium flame.

15. Fry the prepared samosas until light golden brown and cooked through.

16. Remove and drain excess oil.

17. Alternatively, bake the samosas in a preheated oven at 200C for about 30 minutes.

18. Serve hot with mint chutney and ketchup.

Broccoli Samosa

Ingredients:

Maida – 200 Gms

White Chickpeas – 200 Gms, boiled

Broccoli Florets – 1 cup, cleaned, washed, chopped

Green Chillies – 6

Onions – 2, finely chopped

Saunf – 1/4 tsp

Garam Masala Powder – 1 tsp

Ghee – as required

Coriander Leaves – handful, chopped

Salt as per taste

Oil for frying

Method:

1. Combine salt, ghee and maida in a bowl.

2. Mix well to a thick dough.

3. Heat very little oil in a pan.

4. Fry the saunf for 20 to 30 seconds.

5. Add the onions, green chillies, broccoli and chickpeas.

6. Saute for 2 to 3 minutes.

7. Add the garam masala powder, salt and coriander leaves.

8. Stir to mix well. Remove after a minute.

9. Make small balls of the dough and roll them out into small puris.

10. Add 1 or 2 tsp of the broccoli mixture and fold into a triangle.

11. Heat oil for deep frying over medium flame.

12. Fry the prepared samosas till light golden brown and remove.

13. Drain excess oil.

14. Serve with green chutney or ketchup.

Methi Samosa

Ingredients:

Maida – 1 cup

Moong Dal – 1/4 cup, boiled

Onions – 1/2 cup, finely chopped

Methi (Fenugreek Leaves) – half bunch, cleaned, chopped

Butter – 2 tblsp

Baking Powder – 1/4 tsp

Turmeric Powder – 1/2 tsp

Saunf – 1/2 tsp

Ginger Paste – 1/2 tsp

Green Chilli Paste – 1/2 tsp

Dry Mango Powder – 1 tsp

Coriander Powder – 1 tsp

Garam Masala Powder – 1 tsp

Salt as per taste

Method:

1. Combine the methi, cooked dal and salt in a bowl.

2. Mix well and keep aside.

3. Heat oil in a pan over medium flame.

4. Fry the saunf, ginger paste, green chillies and onions for 2 minutes.

5. Add turmeric powder, coriander powder, garam masala powder and dry mango powder.

6. Stir to mix well and add the methi-dal mixture.

7. Cook for a minute and remove.

8. Add baking powder, butter and salt to maida.

9. Pour enough water and knead well to a thick dough.

10. Keep aside for 30 minutes.

11. Make small balls of the mixture and roll them into small puris.

12. Add a spoonful (or more) of the filling to the centre and fold into a triangle.

13. Seal the edges with little water and keep aside.

14. Heat oil in a deep frying pan over medium flame.

15. Fry the prepared samosa till light golden brown.

16. Remove and drain excess oil.

17. Serve with chutney or sauce

Wheat Samosa

Ingredients:

Wheat Flour – 3/4 cup

Maida – 1/4 cup

Butter – 2 tsp

Green Chilli – 1, finely chopped

Ginger – a small piece, finely chopped

Potatoes – 2, boiled, peeled, mashed

Green Peas – 1 tblsp, soaked in water, drained

Red Chilli Powder – 1/2 tsp

Turmeric Powder – 1/4 tsp

Coriander Leaves – 1 tblsp, chopped

Garam Masala Powder – 1/2 tsp

Chaat Masala Powder – 1/2 tsp

Dry Mango Powder (Amchur) – 1/4 tsp

Saunf – 1/2 tsp

Oil as required

Salt as per taste

Method:

1. Combine the wheat flour and maida in a bowl.

2. Add little salt, butter and sprinkle a little water.

3. Knead well to a thick dough and keep aside for 30 minutes.

4. Heat 2 tsp oil in a pan over medium flame.

5. Fry the saunf till golden.

6. Add ginger, green chillies, salt, red chilli powder, turmeric powder, chaat masala powder, garam masala powder and mango powder.

7. Mix well.

8. Add coriander leaves, mashed potatoes and stir well for a minute.

9. Remove the pan from the flame.

10. Make small balls of the mixture and place them on a plate.

11. Make small balls of the dough and flatten them.

12. Place one of the potato balls on the centre and fold over like a samosa.

13. Alternatively, you can shape the dough into a cone and place the potato ball inside. Then fold and seal the edges with little water.

14. Heat oil for frying in a deep pan.

15. Fry the samosas till light golden brown.

16. Remove and drain excess oil.

17. Serve hot with chutney or sauce.

Spinach Vegetable

Ingredients:

Maida – 200 Gms

Ponnanganni Keerai (Greens) – handful, chopped

Onion – 1, chopped

Cabbage – 4 tsp, grated

Carrot – 2 tsp, grated

Potatoes – 2, boiled, peeled, mashed

Oil – 250 ml

Garam Masala Powder as per taste

Salt as per taste

Method:

1. Add a little water and salt to the maida.

2. Mix well to a thick paste.

3. Heat little oil in a pan.

4. Saute the spinach, onion, cabbage and carrot for a few minutes.

5. Remove and transfer to a bowl.

6. Add the mashed potatoes, salt and garam masala powder.

7. Mix well and make small balls of the mixture.

8. Make small balls of the maida and flatten them.

9. Place a portion of the filling and shape them into a samosa.

10. Heat oil for frying over medium flame.

11. Deep fry the prepared samosas till golden brown and crisp.

12. Remove and drain excess oil.

13. Serve with ketchup or chutney of choice.

Moong Sprouts Samosa

Ingredients:

Maida – 1 cup

Ghee as required

Salt as per taste

Oil as required

For the Filling:

Sprouted Green Gram – 1 cup

Potato – 1/4 cup, mashed

Green Peas – 1/4 cup

Carrot – 1/4 cup

Beans – 1/4 cup

Salt as per taste

Red Chilli Powder – as per taste

Method:

1. Mix maida with ghee, salt and oil.

2. Knead to a soft dough using little water.

3. Make balls and roll them into discs.

4. Meanwhile, heat a pan over moderate flame.

5. Add all the vegetables for filling with salt and chilli powder.

6. Cook for a minute or two until well done.

7. Place 1 or 2 tblsp of the cooked vegetables in the centre of the discs.

8. Close in a triangle shape and seal the edges with water.

9. Heat oil in a pan.

10. Fry the samosas till golden brown.

11. Remove and drain excess oil.

12. Serve hot with chutney or ketchup.

Crispy Paneer Samosa

Ingredients:

Paneer – 1 cup, grated

For the Filling:

Oil – 2 tsp

Cumin Seeds – 1 tsp

Green Chillies – 1/2 tblsp, chopped

Onions – 1/4 cup, chopped

Carrots – 1/4 cup, grated

Peas – 1/2 cup, boiled and semi mashed

Potatoes – 1/2 cup, boiled and semi mashed

Cumin Powder – 1/2 tsp

Red Chilli Powder – 1/2 tsp

Chaat Masala – 1/2 tsp

Salt to taste

For the Dough:

Refined Flour – 1 1/2 cups

Oil – 2 tsp

Salt to taste

Water as required

Oil to deep fry

Method:

1. Heat the oil in a pan.

2. Add the cumin seeds and green chillies, then add the onions, carrots, peas and potatoes.

3. Saute for 2 minutes.

4. Stir in the paneer.

5. Season with the cumin and chilli powders, chaat masala and salt.

6. Remove the pan from the stove and keep aside.

7. Put the flour in a bowl along with the oil and salt.

8. Add enough water to make a smooth dough. Knead well.

9. Divide the dough into balls.

10. Flatten and roll out each ball on a floured surface into a saucer-sized circle.

11. Cut into half and form each semi-circle into a cone.

12. Fill the cone with the paneer mixture, wet the open edges with water and press them together to seal them.

13. Heat oil in a kadai and deep fry the samosa till they turn crisp and brown.

14. Remove with a slooted spoon.

15. Drain and serve hot with tomato chutney or green chutney.

Cauliflower Samosa

Ingredients:

Square Spring Roll Wrappers – 1 packet (25cm/10in), thawed if frozen

Plain Flour – 2 tbsp, mixed to a paste with water

Vegetable Oil – for deep frying

Coriander Leaves – to garnish

For the Filling

Ghee or Unsalted Butter – 2 tbsp

Onion – 1 small, finely chopped

Fresh Root Ginger – 1/2 inch piece, chopped

Garlic – 1 clove, crushed

Chilli Powder – 1/2 tsp

Potato – 1 large, cooked and finely diced

Cauliflower Florets – 1/2 cup, lightly cooked and chopped into small pieces

Frozen Peas – 1/2 cup, thawed

Garam Masala – 1 to 2 tsp

Fresh Coriander – 1 tbsp, chopped

Lemon Juice

Salt – as per taste

Method:

1. Heat the ghee or butter in a wok and fry the onion, ginger and garlic for 5 minutes until softened. Add the chilli powder, cook for 1 minute, then stir in the potato, cauliflower and peas.

2. Sprinkle with garam masala and set aside to cool. Stir in the coriander, lemon juice and salt.

3. Cut the spring roll wrappers into three strips. Brush the edges with flour paste. Place a small spoonful of filling about 2cm in from the edge of one strip. Fold one corner over the filling to make a triangle and continue to folding until the entire strip has been used and a triangular pastry has been formed. Seal any open edges with more flour and water paste, adding more water if the paste is very thick.

4. Heat the oil for Deeping to 190C and fry the samosa until golden and crisp.

5. Drain well on kitchen paper and serve hot garnished with coriander leaves and accompanied by cucumber, carrot and celery matchsticks, if you like.

Sweet Samosa

Ingredients:

Maida – 1 cup

Fine Rawa – 1/4 cup

Salt – a pinch

Oil and Vanaspati – for deep frying

For inner filling

Cashewnut – 1/2 cup

Musk melon seeds – 1/2 cup

Powdered sugar – 1 cup

Cardamom powder – little

Method:

1. Mix rawa, maida, salt with enough water to form a thick dough.

2. Keep aside for half an hour closed with wet cloth.

3. Knead well again to make the dough soft and pliable.

4. Dry cashewnuts, melon seeds under hot sun for one hour.

5. Powder separately, and mix together with powdered sugar and cardamom powder.

6. Make small balls from the maida dough and roll it out into very thin chapathis.

7. Put it on top of a greased samosa mould.

8. Spread little filling on top, wet the edges and seal well.

9. Remove samosa from mould and deep fry in oil in reduced flame till crisp and golden

Mushroom Samosa

Ingredients:

Dough

225 gm flour

1/2 tsp salt

4 tbsp oil

4 tbsp water

Filling

2 tbsp oil

1 chopped onion

300 gm diced mushrooms

1 tsp ginger paste

2 chopped green chillies

1/2 tsp garam masala

1/2 tsp ground cumin seeds

2 tbsp chopped coriander

2 tbsp lemon juice

Oil for frying

Salt to taste

Method:

Combine all the dough ingredients and make into stiff dough.

Heat oil in a pan and saute onions.

Add the rest of the filling ingredients and cook until the mushrooms are tender. Sharpen with lemon juice.

Add chopped coriander and seasoning. Cool.

Divide the dough into small balls, roll out into circle and cut into two halves.

Moisten the edges and shape into cones. Fill a teaspoon of the mixture and seal.

Fry the samosa in hot oil until golden in color.

Serve hot with mint chutney.

Cocktail Samosas

Ingredients

For Crust:

Maida- 1 cup

Oil – to fry

1 teaspoon to knead maida.

Salt – to taste.

Take maida in a pan,

Add salt and knead.

(Cover this dough with a wet kitchen napkin until the filling is ready.)

For filling:

Boiled potatoes – 3 or 4

Oil – 2 teaspoon

Onion – 1 v. thin slices

Jeera – 1/2 teaspoon

Salt, turmeric, chilli powder, fresh coriander

Peas (optional)

Chat masala – 1 teaspoon

Method

Heat oil in a pan, add jeera.

Then add onion. After the onions turn transparent, add turmeric, chilli powder, salt and heat for a few more seconds.

Then add the boiled potatoes (smashed). Add peas and green coriander if desired. And the filling is already.

Now, make balls out of the dough (size that of a puri).Cut it into half. Use these 2 halves to make 2 samosas.

Put the filling onto the centre. Fold as a triangle. Fry them.

Arrange them in a plate. Now sprinkle some chat masala on to them. Your samosas are ready... and enjoy the party.

Samosa

Ingredients

For cover:

1 cup plain flour (maida)

2 tbsp. warm oil

Water to knead dough

For filling:

2 potatoes large boiled, peeled, mashed

1 onion finely chopped

2 green chillies crushed

1/2 tsp. ginger crushed

1/2 tsp. garlic crushed

1 tbsp. coriander finely chopped

1/2 lemon juice extracted

1/2 tsp. turmeric powder

1/2 tsp. garam masala

1/2 tsp. coriander seeds cru shed

1 tsp. red chilli powder

Salt to taste

Oil to deep fry

Method:

For dough:

Make well in the flour.

Add oil, salt and little water. Mix well till crumbly.

Add more water little by little, kneading into soft pliable dough.

Cover with moist cloth, keep aside for 15-20 minutes.

Beat dough on work surface and knead again. Re-cover.

For filling:

Heat 3 tbsp. oil, add ginger, green chilli, garlic, coriander seeds.

Stir fry for a minute, add onion, saute till light brown.

Add coriander, lemon, turmeric, salt, red chilli, garam masala.

Stir fry for 2 minutes, add potatoes. Stir further 2 minutes.

Cool. Keep aside.

To proceed:

Make a thin 5″ diam. round with some dough.

Cut into two halves. Run a moist finger along diameter.

Join and press together to make a cone.

Place a tbsp. of filling in the cone and seal third side as above.

Make five to six. Put in hot oil, deep fry on low to medium till light brown.

Do not fry on high, or the samosas will turn out oily and soggy.

Drain on rack or kitchen paper.

Serve hot with green and tamarind chutneys (refer chutneys), or tomato sauce.

Printed in Great Britain
by Amazon

83688849R00020